Impressum
Verlag: BABADADA GmbH, Nedderfeld 112 , 22529 Hamburg
Geschäftsführer / Verlagsleitung: Harald Hof
Druck: Books on Demand GmbH, In de Tarpen 42, 22848 Norderstedt

Imprint
Publisher: BABADADA GmbH, Nedderfeld 112 , 22529 Hamburg, Germany
Managing Director / Publishing direction: Harald Hof
Print: Books on Demand GmbH, In de Tarpen 42, 22848 Norderstedt

classroom
salle de classe

divide
diviser

186/2

board
tableau noir

school yard
cour (de récréation)

teacher
professeur

paper
papier

write
écrire

pen
stylo

desk
bureau

ruler
règle

book
livre

pupil
élève

satchel
cartable

pencil case
trousse

pencil
crayon

pencil sharpener
taille-crayon

rubber
gomme

drawing pad
carnet à dessin

drawing

dessin

paintbrush

pinceau

paint box

boîte de peinture

scissors

ciseaux

glue

colle

exercise book

cahier d'exercices

homework

devoirs

number

chiffre

add

additionner

subtract

soustraire

multiply

multiplier

calculate

calculer

letter

lettre

alphabet

alphabet

word

mot

text
texte

read
lire

chalk
craie

lesson
leçon

register
livre de classe

exam
examen

certificate
certificat

school uniform
uniforme scolaire

education
formation

encyclopedia
lexique

university
université

microscope
microscope

map
carte

waste-paper basket
corbeille à papier

hotel
hôtel

Grand

hostel
auberge

ROOMS

bureau de change
bureau de change

ÉCHANGE

suitcase
valise

car
voiture

language

langue

yes / no

oui / non

Okay

d'accord

hello

Salut

translator

interprète

Thank you

merci

how much is...?

Combien coûte...?

I do not understand

Je ne comprends pas

problem

problème

Good evening!

Bonsoir !

Good morning!

Bonjour !

Good night!

Bonne nuit !

bye bye

Au revoir

direction

direction

luggage

bagages

bag

sac

backpack

sac-à-dos

guest

hôte

room

pièce

sleeping bag

sac de couchage

tent

tente

travel - voyage

tourist information

office de tourisme

beach

plage

credit card

carte de crédit

breakfast

petit-déjeuner

lunch

déjeuner

dinner

dîner

ticket

billet

lift

ascenseur

stamp

timbre

border

frontière

customs

douane

embassy

ambassade

visa

visa

passport

passeport

travel - voyage

aeroplane
avion

ship
navire

fire engine
véhicule de pompiers

bus
bus

truck
camion

motorboat
bateau à moteur

bike
bicyclette

car
voiture

ferry

ferry

boat

barque

motorbike

moto

police car

voiture de police

racing car

voiture de course

rental car

voiture de location

car sharing

auto-partage

breakdown truck

voiture de remorquage

refuse truck

benne à ordures

motor

moteur

fuel

essence

petrol station

station d'essence

traffic sign

panneau indicateur

traffic

trafic

traffic jam

embouteillage

car park

parking

train station

gare

tracks

rails

train

train

tram

tramway

carriage

wagon

helicopter

hélicoptère

airport

aéroport

tower

tour

passenger

passager

container

conteneur

carton

carton

cart

chariot

basket

corbeille

take off / land

décoller / atterrir

city

ville

village

village

city centre

centre-ville

house

maison

cinema
cinéma

advert
publicité

street lamp
réverbère

CINEMA

street
rue

taxi
taxi

snack shop
kiosque

pedestrian
piéton

pavement
trottoir

zebra crossing
passage piéton

bin
poubelle

crossing
carrefour

traffic lights
feux de circulation

hut
....
cabane

flat
....
appartement

train station
....
gare

town hall
....
mairie

museum
....
musée

school
....
école

university

université

bank

banque

hospital

hôpital

hotel

hôtel

pharmacy

pharmacie

office

bureau

book shop

librairie

shop

magasin

florist's

fleuriste

supermarket

supermarché

market

marché

department store

grand magasin

fishmonger's

poissonnerie

shopping centre

centre commercial

harbour

port

park

parc

bench

banque

bridge

pont

stairs

escaliers

underground

métro

tunnel

tunnel

bus stop

arrêt de bus

bar

bar

restaurant

restaurant

postbox

boîte à lettres

street sign

panneau indicateur

parking meter

parcmètre

zoo

zoo

swimming pool

piscine

mosque

mosquée

farm
ferme

pollution
pollution

graveyard
cimetière

church
église

playground
aire de jeux

temple
temple

landscape

paysage

leaf
feuille

signpost
panneau indicateur

way
chemin

meadow
pré

stone
pierre

tree
arbre

hiker
randonneur

river
rivière

grass
herbe

flower
fleur

valley
vallée

hill
montagne

lake
lac

forest
forêt

desert
désert

volcano
volcan

castle
château

rainbow
arc-en-ciel

mushroom
champignon

palm tree
palmier

mosquito
moustique

fly
mouche

ant
fourmis

bee
abeille

spider
araignée

landscape - paysage

beetle

coléoptère

frog

grenouille

squirrel

écureuil

hedgehog

hérisson

hare

lièvre

owl

chouette

bird

oiseau

swan

cygne

boar

sanglier

deer

cerf

moose

élan

dam

barrage

wind turbine

éolienne

solar panel

panneau solaire

climate

climat

waiter
serveur

menu
menu

chair
chaise

soup
soupe

pizza
pizza

tablecloth
nappe

cutlery
couverts

starter

hors d'œuvre

main course

plat principal

dessert

dessert

drinks

boissons

food

alimentation

bottle

bouteille

fast food

fast-food

street food

plats à emporter

teapot

théière

sugar bowl

sucrier

portion

portion

espresso machine

machine à expresso

high chair

chaise haute

bill

facture

tray

plateau

knife

couteau

fork

fourchette

spoon

cuillère

teaspoon

cuillère à thé

serviette

serviette

glass

verre

plate

assiette

soup plate

assiette à soupe

saucer

soucoupe

sauce

sauce

salt pot

salière

pepper mill

moulin à poivre

vinegar

vinaigre

oil

huile

spices

épices

ketchup

ketchup

mustard

moutarde

mayonnaise

mayonnaise

special offer
offre promotionnelle

customer
client

dairy
produits laitiers

fruit
fruits

trolley
chariot

butcher's
boucherie

baker's
boulangerie

weigh
peser

vegetables
légumes

meat
viande

frozen food
aliments surgelés

cold meat

charcuterie

tinned food

conserves

washing powder

poudre à lessive

sweets

bonbons

household products

articles ménagers

cleaning products

détergents

salesperson

vendeuse

till

caisse

cashier

caissier

shopping list

liste d'achats

opening hours

heures d'ouverture

wallet

portefeuille

credit card

carte de crédit

bag

sac

plastic bag

sac en plastique

supermarket - supermarché

21

drinks
boissons

water
eau

juice
jus de fruit

milk
lait

coke
coca

wine
vin

beer
bière

alcohol
alcool

cocoa
chocolat chaud

tea
thé

coffee
café

espresso
expresso

cappuccino
cappuccino

banana

banane

apple

pomme

orange

orange

melon

melon

lemon

citron

carrot

carotte

garlic

ail

bamboo

bambou

onion

oignon

mushroom

champignon

nuts

noisettes

noodles

pâtes

spaghetti

spaghetti

rice

riz

salad

salade

chips

pommes frites

fried potatoes

pommes de terre rôties

pizza

pizza

hamburger

hamburger

sandwich

sandwich

cutlet

escalope

ham

jambon

salami

salami

sausage

saucisse

chicken

poulet

roast

rôti

fish

poisson

porridge oats

flocons d'avoine

muesli

muesli

cornflakes

cornflakes

flour

farine

croissant

croissant

bread roll

petits-pains

bread

pain

toast

pain grillé

biscuits

biscuits

butter

beurre

curd

le fromage blanc

cake

gâteau

egg

œuf

fried egg

œuf au plat

cheese

fromage

ice cream

glace

sugar

sucre

honey

miel

jam

confiture

chocolate spread

crème nougat

curry

curry

farmhouse
ferme

straw bale
botte de paille

barn
grange

field
champ

horse
cheval

trailer
remorque

tractor
tracteur

foal
poulain

donkey
âne

lamb
agneau

sheep
mouton

goat
chèvre

cow
vache

calf
veau

pig
porc

piglet
porcelet

bull
taureau

goose

oie

duck

canard

chick

poussin

hen

poule

cock

coq

rat

rat

cat

chat

mouse

souris

ox

bœuf

dog

chien

doghouse

chenil

garden hose

tuyau de jardin

watering can

arrosoir

scythe

faucheuse

plough

charrue

sickle

faucille

hoe

pioche

pitchfork

fourche

axe

hache

wheelbarrow

brouette

trough

cuve

milk can

pot à lait

sack

sac

fence

clôture

stable

étable

greenhouse

serre

soil

sol

seed

semences

fertilizer

engrais

combine harvester

moissonneuse-batteuse

harvest

récolter

harvest

récolte

yams

igname

wheat

blé

soy

soja

potato

pomme de terre

corn

maïs

rapeseed

colza

fruit tree

arbre fruitier

cassava

manioc

cereals

céréales

chimney
cheminée

roof
toit

drainpipe
gouttière

window
fenêtre

garage
garage

doorbell
sonnette

door
porte

rubbish bin
poubelle

letterbox
boîte aux lettres

garden
jardin

living room
....
salon

bathroom
....
salle de bain

kitchen
....
cuisine

bedroom
....
chambre à coucher

child's room
....
chambre d'enfant

dining room
....
salle à manger

floor

sol

wall

mur

ceiling

plafond

cellar

cave

sauna

sauna

balcony

balcon

terrace

terrasse

pool

piscine

lawn mower

tondeuse à gazon

sheet

housse

bedspread

couette

bed

lit

broom

balai

bucket

sceau

switch

interrupteur

wallpaper
papier peint

picture
image

lamp
lampe

shelf
étagère

cupboard
armoire

television
télé

fireplace
cheminée

flower
fleur

cushion
coussin

sofa
sofa

vase
vase

remote control
télécommande

carpet

tapis

curtain

rideau

table

table

chair

chaise

rocking chair

chaise à bascule

armchair

fauteuil

book

livre

blanket

couverture

decoration

décoration

firewood

bois de chauffage

film

film

hi-fi equipment

chaîne hi-fi

key

clé

newspaper

journal

painting

peinture

poster

poster

radio

radio

notepad

bloc-notes

hoover

aspirateur

cactus

cactus

candle

bougie

fridge
réfrigérateur

microwave oven
four à micro-ondes

kitchen scales
balance de cuisine

toaster
grille-pain

detergent
détergent

freezer
compartiment congélateur

oven
four

rubbish bin
poubelle

dishwasher
lave-vaisselle

cooker
four

pot
casserole

cast-iron pot
marmite

wok / kadai
wok / kadai

pan
poêle

kettle
bouilloire electrique

steamer

cuiseur vapeur

baking tray

plaque de cuisson

crockery

vaisselle

mug

gobelet

bowl

coupe

chopsticks

baguettes

ladle

louche

spatula

spatule

whisk

fouet

strainer

passoire

sieve

tamis

grater

râpe

mortar

mortier

barbecue

barbecue

open fire

cheminée

chopping board

planche à découper

rolling pin

rouleau à pâtisserie

corkscrew

tire-bouchon

can

boîte

can opener

ouvre-boîte

pot holder

maniques

sink

lavabo

brush

brosse

sponge

éponge

blender

mixeur

deep freezer

congélateur

baby bottle

biberon

tap

robinet

heating
chauffage

shower
douche

towel
serviette

shower curtain
rideau de douche

bubble bath
bain moussant

bathtub
baignoire

glass
verre

washing machine
machine à laver

tap
robinet

tiles
carrelage

potty
pot

sink
lavabo

toilet

toilettes

squat toilet

toilette à la turque

bidet

bidet

urinal

urinoir

toilet paper

papier toilette

toilet brush

brosse à toilette

toothbrush

brosse à dents

toothpaste

dentifrice

dental floss

fil dentaire

wash

laver

handheld shower

douche manuelle

douche

douche intime

basin

vasque

back brush

brosse dorsale

soap

savon

shower gel

gel douche

shampoo

shampooing

flannel

gant de toilette

drain

écoulement

cream

crème

deodorant

déodorant

mirror

miroir

hand mirror

miroir cosmétique

razor

rasoir

shaving foam

mousse à raser

aftershave

après-rasage

comb

peigne

brush

brosse

hair dryer

sèche-cheveux

hairspray

laque pour cheveux

makeup

fond de teint

lipstick

rouge à lèvres

nail varnish

vernis à ongles

cotton wool

ouate

nail scissors

coupe-ongles

perfume

parfum

washbag

trousse de toilette

stool

tabouret

weighing scale

pèse-personne

bathrobe

peignoir

rubber gloves

gants de nettoyage

tampon

tampon

sanitary towel

serviettes hygiéniques

chemical toilet

toilette chimique

alarm clock
réveil

cuddly toy
doudou

toy car
voiture jouet

rattle
hochet

doll's house
maison de poupée

present
cadeau

balloon

ballon

bed

lit

pram

poussette

deck of cards

jeu de cartes

jigsaw

puzzle

comic

bande dessinée

lego bricks

pièces lego

building blocks

blocs de construction

action figure

figurine

babygrow

grenouillère

frisbee

frisbee

mobile

mobile

board game

jeu de société

dice

dé

model train set

train miniature

dummy

sucette

party

fête

picture book

livre d'images

ball

balle

doll

poupée

play

jouer

sandpit

bac à sable

swing

balançoire

toys

jouets

video game console

console de jeu

tricycle

tricycle

teddy bear

ours en peluche

wardrobe

armoire

clothing

vêtements

socks

chaussettes

stockings

bas

tights

collant

scarf
écharpe

belt
ceinture

umbrella
parapluie

t-shirt
t-shirt

trainers
baskets

boots
bottes

slippers
pantoufles

sandals
sandales

shoes
chaussures

rubber boots
bottes de caoutchouc

underpants
sous-vêtements

bra
soutien-gorge

vest
maillot de corps

clothing - vêtements

body

body

trousers

pantalon

jeans

jean

skirt

jupe

blouse

chemisier

shirt

chemise

pullover

pull

hoodie

sweat à capuche

blazer

veste

jacket

veste

coat

manteau

raincoat

imperméable

costume

costume

dress

robe

wedding dress

robe de mariée

suit
costume

nightgown
chemise de nuit

pyjamas
pyjama

sari
sari

headscarf
foulard

turban
turban

burqa
burqa

kaftan
caftan

abaya
abaya

swimsuit
maillot de bain

trunks
maillot de bain

shorts
short

tracksuit
tenue d'entraînement

apron
tablier

gloves
gants

button

bouton

glasses

lunettes

bracelet

bracelet

necklace

collier

ring

bague

earring

boucle d'oreille

cap

bonnet

coat hanger

cintre

hat

chapeau

tie

cravate

zip

fermeture éclair

helmet

casque

braces

bretelles

school uniform

uniforme scolaire

uniform

uniforme

bib
bavoir

dummy
sucette

nappy
lange

office

bureau

server
serveur

filing cabinet
armoire d'archivage

printer
imprimante

monitor
écran

paper
papier

mouse
souris

desk
bureau

folder
classeur

keyboard
clavier

waste-paper basket
corbeille à papier

chair
chaise

computer
ordinateur

coffee mug

tasse de café

calculator

calculatrice

internet

internet

laptop

ordinateur portable

letter

lettre

message

message

mobile

portable

network

réseau

photocopier

photocopieuse

software

logiciel

telephone

téléphone

plug socket

prise

fax machine

fax

form

formulaire

document

document

buy

acheter

pay

payer

trade

faire du commerce

money

monnaie

dollar

dollar

euro

euro

yen

yen

rouble

rouble

Swiss franc

franc suisse

renminbi yuan

renminbi yuan

rupee

roupie

cashpoint

distributeur automatique

bureau de change

bureau de change

gold

or

silver

argent

oil

pétrole

energy

énergie

price

prix

contract

contrat

tax

taxe

stock

action

work

travailler

employee

employé

employer

employeur

factory

usine

shop

magasin

police officer
agent de police

fireman
pompier

cook
cuisinier

doctor
médecin

pilot
pilote

gardener

jardinier

carpenter

menuisier

seamstress

couturière

judge

juge

chemist

chimiste

actor

acteur

bus driver

conducteur de bus

taxi driver

chauffeur de taxi

fisherman

pêcheur

cleaning lady

femme de ménage

roofer

couvreur

waiter

serveur

hunter

chasseur

painter

peintre

baker

boulanger

electrician

électricien

builder

ouvrier

engineer

ingénieur

butcher

boucher

plumber

plombier

postman

facteur

soldier

soldat

architect

architecte

cashier

caissier

florist

fleuriste

hairdresser

coiffeur

conductor

contrôleur

mechanic

mécanicien

captain

capitaine

dentist

dentiste

scientist

scientifique

rabbi

rabbin

imam

imam

monk

moine

clergyman

prêtre

hammer
marteau

pliers
pinces

screwdriver
tournevis

spanner
clé

torch
torche

digger
pelleteuse

toolbox
boîte à outils

ladder
échelle

saw
scie

nails
clous

drill
perceuse

tools - outils

repair
....
réparer

shovel
....
pelle

Damn!
....
Mince !

dustpan
....
pelle

paint pot
....
pot de peinture

screws
....
vis

musical instruments
instruments de musique

loudspeaker
haut-parleurs

drum kit
batterie

guitar
guitare

double bass
contrebasse

trumpet
trompette

piano

piano

violin

violon

bass

basse

timpani

timbales

drums

tambour

keyboard

piano électrique

saxophone

saxophone

flute

flûte

microphone

microphone

entrance
entrée

tiger
tigre

cage
cage

zebra
zèbre

animal feed
alimentation animale

panda
panda

animals
animaux

elephant
éléphant

kangaroo
kangourou

rhino
rhinocéros

gorilla
gorille

bear
ours

camel

chameau

ostrich

autruche

lion

lion

monkey

singe

flamingo

flamand rose

parrot

perroquet

polar bear

ours polaire

penguin

pingouin

shark

requin

peacock

paon

snake

serpent

crocodile

crocodile

zookeeper

gardien de zoo

seal

phoque

jaguar

jaguar

pony

poney

leopard

léopard

hippo

hippopotame

giraffe

girafe

eagle

aigle

boar

sanglier

fish

poisson

turtle

tortue

walrus

morse

fox

renard

gazelle

gazelle

American football
american Football

cycling
cyclisme

tennis
tennis

basketball
basket-ball

swimming
natation

boxing
boxe

ice hockey
hockey sur glace

football
football

badminton
badminton

athletics
athlétisme

handball
handball

skiing
ski

polo
polo

jump
sauter

hug
embrasser

laugh
rire

walk
marcher

sing
chanter

dream
rêver

pray
prier

kiss
faire la bise

write
écrire

draw
dessiner

show
montrer

push
pousser

give
donner

take
prendre

have
avoir

do
faire

be
être

stand
être debout

run
courir

pull
trier

throw
jeter

fall
tomber

lie
être couché

wait
attendre

carry
porter

sit
être assis

get dressed
s'habiller

sleep
dormir

wake up
se réveiller

look at

regarder

cry

pleurer

stroke

caresser

comb

peigner

talk

parler

understand

comprendre

ask

demander

listen

écouter

drink

boire

eat

manger

tidy up

ranger

love

aimer

cook

cuire

drive

conduire

fly

voler

activities - activités

sail

faire de la voile

calculate

calculer

read

lire

learn

apprendre

work

travailler

marry

se marier

sew

coudre

brush teeth

brosser les dents

kill

tuer

smoke

fumer

send

envoyer

activities - activités

grandmother
grand-mère

grandfather
grand-père

father
père

mother
mère

baby
bébé

daughter
fille

son
fils

guest

hôte

aunt

tante

uncle

oncle

brother

frère

sister

sœur

forehead
front

eye
œil

shoulder
épaule

finger
doigt

face
visage

chin
menton

hand
main

breast
poitrine

leg
jambe

arm
bras

baby

bébé

man

homme

woman

femme

girl

fille

boy

garçon

head

tête

back

dos

belly

ventre

belly button

nombril

toe

orteil

heel

talon

bone

os

hip

hanche

knee

genou

elbow

coude

nose

nez

bottom

fesses

skin

peau

cheek

joue

ear

oreille

lip

lèvre

mouth

bouche

tooth

dent

tongue

langue

brain

cerveau

heart

cœur

muscle

muscle

lung

poumons

liver

foie

stomach

estomac

kidneys

reins

sex

rapport sexuel

condom

préservatif

ovum

ovule

semen

sperme

pregnancy

grossesse

menstruation
menstruation

vagina
vagin

penis
pénis

eyebrow
sourcil

hair
cheveux

neck
cou

hospital
hôpital

ambulance
ambulance

wheelchair
fauteuil roulant

fracture
fracture

doctor

médecin

emergency room

service des urgences

nurse

infirmière

emergency

urgence

unconscious

inconscient

pain

douleur

injury

blessure

bleeding

hémorragie

heart attack

crise cardiaque

stroke

attaque cérébrale

allergy

allergie

cough

toux

fever

fièvre

flu

grippe

diarrhoea

diarrhée

headache

mal de tête

cancer

cancer

diabetes

diabète

surgeon

chirurgien

scalpel

scalpel

operation

opération

CT
CT

x-ray
radiographie

ultrasound
échographie

face mask
masque

disease
maladie

waiting room
salle d'attente

crutch
béquille

plaster
pansement

bandage
pansement

injection
injection

stethoscope
stéthoscope

stretcher
brancard

clinical thermometer
thermomètre

birth
accouchement

overweight
surcharge pondérale

hearing aid

appareil auditif

disinfectant

désinfectant

infection

infection

virus

virus

HIV / AIDS

VIH / sida

medicine

médicament

vaccination

vaccination

tablets

comprimés

pill

pilule

emergency call

appel d'urgence

blood pressure monitor

tensiomètre

ill / healthy

malade / sain

Help!

Au secours !

assault

assaut

alarm

alarme

attack

attaque

danger

danger

emergency exit

sortie de secours

Fire!

Au feu!

fire extinguisher

extincteur

accident

accident

first-aid kit

trousse de premier secours

SOS

SOS

police

police

Europe

Europe

North America

Amérique du Nord

South America

Amérique du Sud

Africa

Afrique

Asia

Asie

Australia

Australie

Atlantic

Océan atlantique

Pacific

Océan pacifique

Indian Ocean

Océan indien

Antarctic Ocean

Océan antarctique

Arctic Ocean

Océan arctique

North Pole

pôle nord

South Pole
pôle sud

Antarctica
Antarctique

Earth
terre

land
pays

sea
mer

island
île

nation
nation

state
état

clock face
....
cadran

hour hand
....
aiguille des heures

minute hand
....
aiguille des minutes

second hand
....
aiguille des secondes

What time is it?
....
Quelle heure est-il ?

day
....
jour

time
....
temps

now
....
maintenant

digital watch
....
montre digitale

minute
....
minute

hour
....
heure

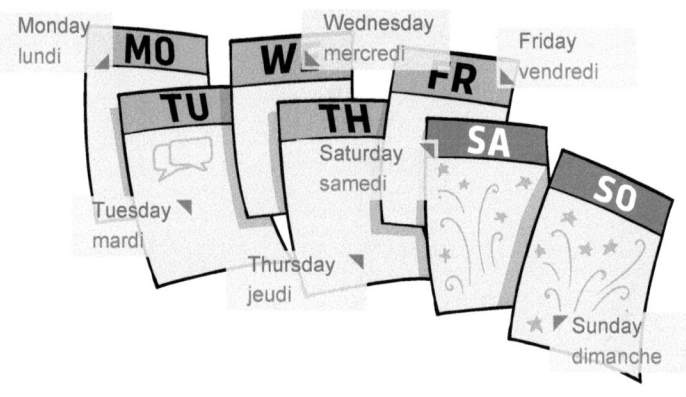

Monday — lundi
Wednesday — mercredi
Friday — vendredi
Tuesday — mardi
Saturday — samedi
Thursday — jeudi
Sunday — dimanche

yesterday

hier

today

aujourd'hui

tomorrow

demain

morning

matin

noon

midi

evening

soir

business days

jours ouvrables

weekend

week-end

rain
pluie

rainbow
arc-en-ciel

snow
neige

wind
vent

spring
printemps

autumn
automne

summer
été

winter
hiver

weather forecast
·················
météo

thermometer
·················
thermomètre

sunshine
·················
lumière du soleil

cloud
·················
nuage

fog
·················
brouillard

humidity
·················
humidité

lightning

foudre

thunder

tonnerre

storm

tempête

hail

grêle

monsoon

mousson

flood

inondation

ice

glace

January

janvier

February

février

March

mars

April

avril

May

mai

June

juin

July

juillet

August

août

September
....
septembre

October
....
octobre

November
....
novembre

December
....
décembre

circle
....
cercle

square
....
carré

rectangle
....
rectangle

triangle
....
triangle

sphere
....
sphère

cube
....
cube

white

blanc

yellow

jaune

orange

orange

pink

rose

red

rouge

purple

violet

blue

bleu

green

vert

brown

marron

grey

gris

black

noir

a lot / a little

beaucoup / peu

angry / calm

fâché / calme

beautiful / ugly

joli / laid

beginning / end

début / fin

big / small

grand / petit

bright / dark

clair / obscure

brother / sister

frère / soeur

clean / dirty

propre / sale

complete / incomplete

complet / incomplet

day / night

jour / nuit

dead / alive

mort / vivant

wide / narrow

large / étroit

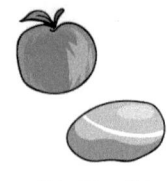

edible / inedible

comestible / incomestible

evil / kind

méchant / gentil

excited / bored

excité / ennuyé

fat / thin

gros / mince

first / last

premier / dernier

friend / enemy

ami / ennemi

full / empty

plein / vide

hard / soft

dur / souple

heavy / light

lourd / léger

hunger / thirst

faim / soif

ill / healthy

malade / sain

illegal / legal

illégal / légal

intelligent / stupid

intelligent / stupide

left / right

gauche / droite

near / far

proche / loin

opposites - oppositions

new / used

nouveau / usé

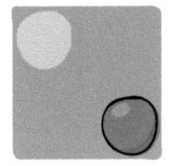

nothing / something

rien / quelque chose

old / young

vieux / jeune

on / off

marche / arrêt

open / closed

ouvert / fermé

quiet / loud

faible / fort

rich / poor

riche / pauvre

right / wrong

correct / incorrect

rough / smooth

rugueux / lisse

sad / happy

triste / heureux

short / long

court / long

slow / fast

lent / rapide

wet / dry

mouillé / sec

warm / cool

chaud / froid

war / peace

guerre / paix

numbers

nombres

0

zero

zéro

1

one

un / une

2

two

deux

3

three

trois

4

four

quatre

5

five

cinq

6

six

six

7

seven

sept

8

eight

huit

9

nine

neuf

10

ten

dix

11

eleven

onze

12
twelve
douze

13
thirteen
treize

14
fourteen
quatorze

15
fifteen
quinze

16
sixteen
seize

17
seventeen
dix-sept

18
eighteen
dix-huit

19
nineteen
dix-neuf

20
twenty
vingt

100
hundred
cent

1.000
thousand
mille

1.000.000
million
million

numbers - nombres

languages

langues

English

anglais

American English

anglais américain

Chinese Mandarin

chinois mandarin

Hindi

hindi

Spanish

espagnol

French

français

Arabic

arabe

Russian

russe

Portuguese

portugais

Bengali

bengali

German

allemand

Japanese

japonais

I
je

you
tu

he / she / it
il / elle / ce, c', cela

we
nous

you
vous

they
ils / elles

who?
Qui ?

what?
Quoi ?

how?
Comment ?

where?
Où ?

when?
Quand ?

name
nom

behind

derrière

in

dans

in front of

devant

over

au-dessus

on

sur

under

en-dessous

beside

à côté de

between

entre

place

lieu